The Women's Suffrage Movement:

American history, Volume 18

Michael Johnson

Published by Harmony House Publishing, 2024.

While every precaution has been taken in the preparation of this book, the publisher assumes no responsibility for errors or omissions, or for damages resulting from the use of the information contained herein.

THE WOMEN'S SUFFRAGE MOVEMENT:

First edition. April 5, 2024.

Copyright © 2024 Michael Johnson.

ISBN: 979-8224677474

Written by Michael Johnson.

Table of Contents

Chapter 1: Introduction to the Women's Suffrage Movement 1

Chapter 2: Early Pioneers and Advocates 4

Chapter 3: The Fight for Suffrage in the 19th Century 8

Chapter 4: Women's Suffrage Organizations.. 12

Chapter 5: Intersectionality and Diversity in the Suffrage Movement........ 16

Chapter 6: State-by-State Campaigns 20

Chapter 7: Suffrage and the Progressive Era....................................... 23

Chapter 8: Suffrage and World War I 26

Chapter 9: The Final Push: Tactics and Strategies 30

Chapter 10: The 19th Amendment.. 33

Chapter 11: Challenges and Achievements After Suffrage 37

Chapter 12: Legacy of the Suffrage Movement 40

Chapter 13: Global Perspectives on Women's Suffrage......................... 44

Chapter 14: Unfinished Business: Continuing Struggles for Equality........ 48

Chapter 15: Conclusion: Looking Forward.. 51

"To the brave suffragists who dared to dream of a more just and equitable society,

This book is dedicated to the trailblazing women and allies who tirelessly fought for women's right to vote. Your unwavering dedication, perseverance, and unwavering commitment to equality paved the way for generations to come. May your legacy inspire us to continue striving for a world where every voice is heard and every person is treated with dignity and respect.

With deepest gratitude and admiration,

Michael Johnson"

Chapter 1: Introduction to the Women's Suffrage Movement

In the annals of American history, few movements have been as transformative and impactful as the Women's Suffrage Movement. This chapter serves as a gateway into the complex tapestry of events, ideologies, and individuals that shaped this monumental struggle for equality.

Historical Context: Women's Rights in the 19th and Early 20th Centuries

To understand the Women's Suffrage Movement, one must first grasp the prevailing societal norms and legal frameworks that constrained women's rights during the 19th and early 20th centuries. In the 1800s, American society operated under a patriarchal system that relegated women to the private sphere, confining them to domestic roles as wives and mothers. Women lacked legal rights, including the right to vote, own property, or pursue higher education. Their voices were systematically silenced, and their agency was severely limited.

The legal status of women was enshrined in state laws and common law doctrines derived from English jurisprudence. The doctrine of coverture, for example, dictated that upon marriage, a woman's legal identity was subsumed by her husband's, rendering her essentially invisible in the eyes of the law. Women had no independent right to enter into contracts, sue or be sued, or control their own earnings. This legal subordination reinforced broader cultural attitudes that positioned women as inherently inferior to men, both intellectually and morally.

The early 19th century saw nascent stirrings of discontent among women who chafed against these restrictions. A few brave voices began to question the status quo, advocating for expanded rights and opportunities for women. However, these early efforts were often met with skepticism, ridicule, or outright hostility from mainstream society.

Key Figures and Events: Pioneers of the Suffrage Movement

The seeds of the Women's Suffrage Movement were sown in the fertile soil of discontent and aspiration. Among the towering figures who laid the groundwork for this movement were Elizabeth Cady Stanton, Lucretia Mott, and Susan B. Anthony.

Elizabeth Cady Stanton, a brilliant writer and orator, emerged as one of the most influential advocates for women's rights in the 19th century. Inspired by her experiences as a wife and mother, Stanton penned the groundbreaking "Declaration of Sentiments" for the Seneca Falls Convention in 1848. Modeled after the Declaration of Independence, this document boldly proclaimed that "all men and women are created equal" and demanded equal rights and opportunities for women in all spheres of life.

Lucretia Mott, a Quaker minister and abolitionist, lent her formidable intellect and moral authority to the cause of women's rights. Alongside Stanton, she organized the historic Seneca Falls Convention, which marked the birth of the American women's rights movement. Mott's unwavering commitment to justice and equality inspired generations of activists to follow in her footsteps.

Susan B. Anthony, perhaps the most iconic figure of the suffrage movement, dedicated her life to the pursuit of women's rights. Fiercely determined and unapologetically outspoken, Anthony traveled the country tirelessly, delivering impassioned speeches and rallying support for the cause. She famously declared, "I declare to you that woman must not depend upon the protection of man, but must be taught to protect herself."

The Seneca Falls Convention of 1848 stands as a seminal moment in the history of the suffrage movement. Convened by Stanton, Mott, and other leading suffragists, this gathering brought together hundreds of men and women from across the country to discuss the social, civil, and religious rights of women. The convention culminated in the adoption of the Declaration of Sentiments, which called for women's suffrage among other demands for equality.

Conclusion

As we embark on this journey through the Women's Suffrage Movement, it is essential to recognize the historical context and the individuals who paved the way for change. The struggles and triumphs of Elizabeth Cady Stanton, Lucretia

Mott, Susan B. Anthony, and countless other unsung heroes serve as a testament to the power of resilience, perseverance, and collective action. In the chapters that follow, we will delve deeper into the intricacies of the suffrage movement, exploring its challenges, victories, and enduring legacy in the ongoing fight for gender equality.

Chapter 2: Early Pioneers and Advocates

In the early 19th century, amidst the backdrop of a society that relegated women to subordinate roles, a group of courageous individuals emerged to challenge the status quo and pave the way for the Women's Suffrage Movement. Among these early pioneers were Elizabeth Cady Stanton, Lucretia Mott, and Susan B. Anthony. Their tireless advocacy, indomitable spirit, and unwavering commitment to equality laid the foundation for one of the most consequential social movements in American history.

Elizabeth Cady Stanton: The Philosopher of Women's Rights

Elizabeth Cady Stanton, born on November 12, 1815, in Johnstown, New York, was a visionary thinker and eloquent advocate for women's rights. From a young age, Stanton rebelled against the limitations imposed on women by society, eagerly devouring her father's law books and dreaming of a world where women enjoyed the same rights and opportunities as men.

Stanton's journey into activism began in earnest when she met Lucretia Mott at the World Anti-Slavery Convention in London in 1840. Inspired by Mott's impassioned advocacy for women's rights, Stanton resolved to dedicate her life to the cause of gender equality.

In 1848, Stanton took a bold step forward by organizing the historic Seneca Falls Convention in Seneca Falls, New York. Alongside Lucretia Mott and other leading suffragists, Stanton penned the "Declaration of Sentiments," a revolutionary document that echoed the language of the Declaration of Independence and called for equal rights and opportunities for women in all spheres of life.

Stanton's intellectual prowess and rhetorical skill made her a formidable leader in the suffrage movement. She fearlessly challenged prevailing notions of gender and power, arguing that women were entitled to full political and civil rights. Stanton's groundbreaking speeches and writings, including her seminal work "The Woman's Bible," laid the groundwork for feminist thought and activism for generations to come.

Lucretia Mott: The Quaker Minister and Abolitionist

Lucretia Mott, born on January 3, 1793, in Nantucket, Massachusetts, was a pioneering Quaker minister and staunch advocate for women's rights and abolition. Raised in a devoutly religious Quaker household, Mott imbibed the values of equality, justice, and nonviolence from an early age.

Mott's involvement in the anti-slavery movement brought her into contact with Elizabeth Cady Stanton, forging a deep and enduring friendship that would shape the course of both their lives. Together, Mott and Stanton organized the Seneca Falls Convention, where Mott delivered a stirring address on the rights of women, challenging the assembled delegates to recognize the inherent dignity and worth of all individuals, regardless of gender.

Mott's commitment to nonviolent resistance and moral integrity served as a guiding light for the suffrage movement. Despite facing ridicule and condemnation from detractors, she remained steadfast in her belief that women possessed the same innate rights and capacities as men. Mott's legacy as a pioneering feminist, abolitionist, and advocate for social justice endures to this day, inspiring countless individuals to strive for a more equitable and inclusive world.

Susan B. Anthony: The Fearless Crusader for Women's Rights

Susan B. Anthony, born on February 15, 1820, in Adams, Massachusetts, emerged as one of the most iconic figures of the suffrage movement. Fiercely independent and unapologetically outspoken, Anthony dedicated her life to the pursuit of women's rights, earning her the nickname "The Napoleon of the Women's Rights Movement."

From a young age, Anthony rebelled against the constraints imposed on women by society, refusing to conform to traditional gender roles. Inspired by the abolitionist movement and her friendship with Elizabeth Cady Stanton, Anthony threw herself into the fight for women's suffrage with unmatched zeal and determination.

Anthony's activism took many forms, from organizing petition drives and delivering fiery speeches to defying unjust laws and social norms. In 1872, she made headlines by daring to cast a ballot in the presidential election, an act of civil disobedience that landed her in jail but galvanized public support for the suffrage cause.

Throughout her life, Anthony remained steadfast in her belief that women were entitled to full political and civil rights. She tirelessly traveled the country, spreading the message of women's suffrage and rallying support for the cause. Anthony's tireless advocacy and indomitable spirit helped to propel the suffrage movement forward, laying the groundwork for the eventual passage of the 19th Amendment.

The Seneca Falls Convention: A Turning Point in Women's History

The Seneca Falls Convention, held on July 19-20, 1848, in Seneca Falls, New York, stands as a watershed moment in the history of the suffrage movement. Organized by Elizabeth Cady Stanton, Lucretia Mott, and other leading suffragists, the convention brought together nearly 300 men and women from across the country to discuss the social, civil, and religious rights of women.

The convention began with a stirring address by Lucretia Mott, who exhorted the assembled delegates to recognize the inherent dignity and worth of women and to support their demand for equal rights. This set the stage for the adoption of the "Declaration of Sentiments," a revolutionary document that boldly proclaimed that "all men and women are created equal" and called for an end to the legal and social subordination of women.

Central to the Declaration of Sentiments was the demand for women's suffrage, which was seen as the cornerstone of women's liberation. The declaration declared that "it is the duty of the women of this country to secure to themselves their sacred right to the elective franchise." This call to action galvanized the delegates and ignited a spark that would ignite the suffrage movement across the nation.

The significance of the Seneca Falls Convention cannot be overstated. It was the first time in American history that women publicly demanded the right to vote, laying the groundwork for future activism and advocacy. While the convention was met with ridicule and opposition from many quarters, it also inspired a new generation of activists to join the fight for women's rights.

Conclusion

As we reflect on the lives and legacies of Elizabeth Cady Stanton, Lucretia Mott, and Susan B. Anthony, we are reminded of the power of courage, conviction, and collective action. These early pioneers and advocates for women's rights dared to dream of a world where women were treated as equals and fought tirelessly to make that dream a reality. Their contributions to the suffrage movement laid the foundation for generations of activists to come, inspiring us to continue the fight for equality and justice for all.

Chapter 3: The Fight for Suffrage in the 19th Century

The 19th century witnessed the emergence of the Women's Suffrage Movement as a potent force for social change in the United States. In this chapter, we delve into the strategies and tactics employed by suffragists during this tumultuous period, as well as the formidable opposition they faced from entrenched interests and societal norms.

Strategies and Tactics of Suffragists

Petitions and Lobbying Efforts

One of the earliest and most enduring tactics utilized by suffragists was the submission of petitions to state legislatures and Congress. Petitions served as a means of voicing women's demands for suffrage and garnering public support for their cause. Suffragists painstakingly collected signatures from women and sympathetic men, often circulating petitions door-to-door or at public gatherings.

Petitions were accompanied by lobbying efforts, as suffragists sought to persuade lawmakers of the justice and necessity of granting women the right to vote. They organized meetings with legislators, wrote letters, and published articles in newspapers and magazines to advance their cause. While initially met with skepticism and resistance, these lobbying efforts gradually gained traction as public opinion began to shift in favor of suffrage.

Lectures and Public Speaking

Suffragists recognized the power of education and persuasion in advancing their cause, and many prominent leaders embarked on lecture tours to spread the message of women's suffrage far and wide. Elizabeth Cady Stanton, Susan B. Anthony, and other leading suffragists crisscrossed the country, delivering impassioned speeches to packed audiences in town halls, lecture halls, and churches.

These lectures served multiple purposes: they educated the public about the injustices faced by women, rebutted arguments against suffrage, and inspired ordinary men and women to join the fight for equality. Suffragists used rhetoric and logic to dismantle stereotypes and misconceptions about women's abilities and suitability for political participation, challenging audiences to reconsider their preconceived notions.

Civil Disobedience and Direct Action

As the suffrage movement gained momentum, some activists turned to more confrontational tactics to demand change. Civil disobedience and direct action became increasingly common, as suffragists staged protests, pickets, and acts of nonviolent resistance to draw attention to their cause.

One of the most notable examples of civil disobedience was the 1913 Woman Suffrage Procession in Washington, D.C., organized by Alice Paul and the National Woman's Party. Thousands of suffragists from across the country marched down Pennsylvania Avenue, demanding the right to vote. The procession was met with hostility and violence from anti-suffrage crowds, but it succeeded in capturing the nation's attention and galvanizing support for the suffrage cause.

Legal Challenges and Test Cases

In addition to grassroots organizing and public advocacy, suffragists pursued legal avenues to secure women's suffrage. They filed lawsuits and test cases challenging discriminatory voting laws and practices, arguing that such laws violated women's constitutional rights.

One of the most famous legal challenges was the case of Minor v. Happersett (1875), in which Virginia Minor sued for the right to vote under the Fourteenth Amendment. The Supreme Court ultimately ruled against Minor, holding that citizenship did not confer the right to vote and that states had the authority to determine voter qualifications.

Despite setbacks in the courts, suffragists continued to press for legal reforms and challenge discriminatory laws at the state and federal levels. Their efforts laid the groundwork for future legal victories and the eventual passage of the 19th Amendment.

Opposition Faced by Suffragists

Political Opposition

The fight for women's suffrage was not without its detractors, and suffragists faced fierce opposition from politicians, party leaders, and special interest groups. Many male politicians viewed women's suffrage as a threat to their power and privilege, fearing that enfranchising women would dilute the influence of male voters and disrupt the existing political order.

Opponents of suffrage argued that women were inherently unfit for political participation, lacking the intelligence, rationality, and temperament necessary to make informed decisions at the ballot box. They also raised concerns about the potential impact of suffrage on family dynamics and social stability, warning of the breakdown of traditional gender roles and the erosion of moral values.

Social and Cultural Attitudes

Suffragists also faced resistance from broader societal attitudes and cultural norms that upheld the primacy of male authority and the sanctity of the domestic sphere. Many Americans, both men and women, believed that women's place was in the home, caring for their families and tending to domestic duties, rather than engaging in the rough and tumble world of politics.

Moreover, suffragists were often depicted in the media as unfeminine, radical, and even dangerous, reinforcing stereotypes and stigmatizing women who dared to challenge the status quo. Cartoons, caricatures, and editorial cartoons lampooned suffragists as mannish, shrill, and unattractive, seeking to undermine their credibility and delegitimize their demands.

Conclusion

The fight for women's suffrage in the 19th century was marked by a combination of perseverance, ingenuity, and resilience in the face of formidable obstacles. Suffragists employed a variety of strategies and tactics, from petitioning and public speaking to civil disobedience and legal challenges, to advance their cause and secure equal rights for women.

Yet, their efforts were met with staunch opposition from political adversaries, entrenched interests, and societal norms that upheld gender hierarchy and male supremacy. Suffragists confronted ridicule, discrimination, and violence as they pressed forward, undeterred by setbacks and determined to achieve their goals.

In the chapters that follow, we will explore the continued evolution of the suffrage movement in the 20th century, as suffragists intensified their efforts and ultimately triumphed in securing the passage of the 19th Amendment.

Chapter 4: Women's Suffrage Organizations

Throughout the late 19th and early 20th centuries, women's suffrage organizations played a pivotal role in the struggle for women's right to vote in the United States. In this chapter, we will explore two of the most prominent organizations of the era: the National American Woman Suffrage Association (NAWSA) and the National Woman's Party (NWP). We will examine their origins, leadership, strategies, and contributions to the suffrage movement.

The National American Woman Suffrage Association (NAWSA)

Origins and Formation

The National American Woman Suffrage Association (NAWSA) emerged from the merger of two leading suffrage organizations: the National Woman Suffrage Association (NWSA) and the American Woman Suffrage Association (AWSA). The NWSA, led by Elizabeth Cady Stanton and Susan B. Anthony, advocated for a broader vision of women's rights, including suffrage and other civil liberties. In contrast, the AWSA, led by Lucy Stone and Henry Blackwell, focused primarily on securing suffrage rights for women through state-level campaigns.

In 1890, the two organizations merged to form the NAWSA, uniting their efforts and resources in pursuit of a common goal: achieving women's suffrage nationwide. The merger represented a significant milestone in the suffrage movement, consolidating disparate factions and fostering greater cohesion and collaboration among suffragists.

Leadership and Key Figures

The leadership of the NAWSA was characterized by a diverse array of talented and dedicated suffragists, including both veteran activists and rising stars in the movement. Elizabeth Cady Stanton and Susan B. Anthony, two of the most iconic figures in the suffrage movement, played instrumental roles in shaping the organization's agenda and strategy. Stanton's incisive intellect and radical vision, combined with Anthony's tireless activism and organizational skills, provided the NAWSA with dynamic and effective leadership.

Other key figures within the NAWSA included Carrie Chapman Catt, Anna Howard Shaw, and Alice Stone Blackwell, among others. Catt, who succeeded Susan B. Anthony as president of the NAWSA in 1900, brought a strategic acumen and organizational savvy to the organization, steering it through a period of significant growth and expansion. Shaw, a charismatic speaker and gifted organizer, served as president of the NAWSA from 1904 to 1915, bringing her considerable talents to bear in mobilizing support for suffrage at the grassroots level. Blackwell, the daughter of Lucy Stone and Henry Blackwell, inherited her parents' commitment to the cause of women's rights and played a leading role in advancing suffrage through her work with the NAWSA and other organizations.

Strategies and Tactics

The NAWSA employed a multifaceted approach to advancing the cause of women's suffrage, combining legislative advocacy, public education, and grassroots organizing to build support and momentum for reform.

Legislative Advocacy: At the heart of the NAWSA's strategy was a relentless focus on securing suffrage through legislative means. The organization lobbied state legislatures and Congress, urging lawmakers to pass laws granting women the right to vote. NAWSA activists also worked to elect sympathetic candidates to political office, believing that a friendly political climate was essential for achieving their goals.

Public Education: Recognizing the importance of public opinion in shaping policy decisions, the NAWSA undertook extensive public education campaigns to raise awareness about the need for women's suffrage. Suffrage speakers crisscrossed the country, delivering lectures, organizing rallies, and distributing literature to educate the public about the benefits of extending suffrage to women. The organization also utilized newspapers, magazines, and other media outlets to disseminate its message and counter opposition to suffrage.

Grassroots Organizing: The NAWSA mobilized a vast network of grassroots activists, known as "suffrage soldiers," to build support for suffrage at the local level. These activists organized suffrage clubs, held public meetings, and engaged in door-to-door canvassing to recruit supporters and generate enthusiasm for the cause. Grassroots organizing was particularly effective in states where suffrage campaigns were underway, helping to galvanize public support and pressure lawmakers to act.

The National Woman's Party (NWP)

Origins and Formation

The National Woman's Party (NWP) was founded in 1913 by Alice Paul and Lucy Burns, two dynamic and determined suffragists who sought to adopt more militant tactics in the fight for women's suffrage. Dissatisfied with the incremental approach favored by the NAWSA, Paul and Burns believed that more aggressive tactics, such as protests, pickets, and civil disobedience, were necessary to force the issue of suffrage onto the national agenda.

Leadership and Key Figures

Alice Paul emerged as the driving force behind the NWP, bringing a boldness and strategic vision to the suffrage movement that set her apart from her contemporaries. A graduate of Swarthmore College and the University of Pennsylvania, Paul was deeply influenced by the militant suffrage tactics she encountered during a stint in England, where she became involved with the Women's Social and Political Union (WSPU) led by Emmeline Pankhurst.

Joining forces with Lucy Burns and other like-minded activists, Paul spearheaded a campaign of civil disobedience and direct action aimed at pressuring President Woodrow Wilson and Congress to support women's suffrage. The NWP quickly gained a reputation for its bold and confrontational tactics, staging protests, pickets, and hunger strikes to draw attention to the suffrage cause.

Strategies and Tactics

The NWP's approach to suffrage activism was marked by its willingness to challenge authority and disrupt the status quo through nonviolent resistance and civil disobedience.

Protests and Pickets: One of the most visible and controversial tactics employed by the NWP was the staging of protests and pickets outside the White House and other government buildings. Beginning in January 1917, suffragists affiliated with the NWP held daily pickets outside the White House, bearing banners and signs demanding the right to vote. These pickets, known as the "Silent Sentinels," drew widespread attention and generated public sympathy for the suffrage cause.

Hunger Strikes: In addition to picketing, NWP activists engaged in hunger strikes as a form of protest against their imprisonment for engaging in suffrage-related activities. Many suffragists endured harsh treatment and brutal force-feeding while on hunger strike, but their courage and sacrifice captured the public's imagination and galvanized support for suffrage.

Conclusion

The National American Woman Suffrage Association (NAWSA) and the National Woman's Party (NWP) represented two distinct but complementary approaches to suffrage activism in the United States. While the NAWSA focused primarily on legislative advocacy and grassroots organizing, the NWP adopted more militant tactics, including protests, pickets, and hunger strikes, to pressure the government to grant women the right to vote.

Despite their differences, both organizations played a crucial role in advancing the cause of women's suffrage and ultimately achieving success with the passage of the 19th Amendment in 1920. Their leadership, strategies, and sacrifices paved the way for future generations of women to participate fully in the democratic process and helped to lay the foundation for the modern women's rights movement.

Chapter 5: Intersectionality and Diversity in the Suffrage Movement

The history of the Women's Suffrage Movement in the United States is often portrayed through the lens of white, middle-class women, with figures like Susan B. Anthony and Elizabeth Cady Stanton taking center stage. However, the reality is far more complex and nuanced, as the suffrage movement was marked by a rich tapestry of diverse voices and experiences. In this chapter, we will explore the intersectionality within the suffrage movement, including the involvement of women of color and working-class women, and examine the challenges faced by marginalized groups within the movement.

Intersectionality and the Suffrage Movement

Women of Color in the Suffrage Movement

Women of color played a vital but often overlooked role in the suffrage movement, contributing their voices, talents, and leadership to the struggle for equality. African American women, in particular, were active participants in the suffrage movement, organizing their own clubs and associations to advocate for suffrage and civil rights.

One of the most prominent African American suffragists was Sojourner Truth, a former slave and abolitionist who became a powerful advocate for women's rights. Truth's famous "Ain't I a Woman?" speech, delivered at the 1851 Women's Rights Convention in Akron, Ohio, highlighted the intersectional struggles faced by women of color, challenging prevailing notions of womanhood and demanding recognition and respect for their contributions to society.

Other notable African American suffragists included Mary Church Terrell, Ida B. Wells, and Mary Ann Shadd Cary, among others. These women worked tirelessly to challenge racial and gender discrimination, often facing hostility and marginalization within the suffrage movement itself. Despite these challenges, they persisted in their quest for justice and equality, leaving an indelible mark on the suffrage movement and the broader struggle for civil rights.

Working-Class Women in the Suffrage Movement

Working-class women also played a significant role in the suffrage movement, organizing labor unions, strikes, and protests to demand better working conditions and economic opportunities. Many working-class women saw suffrage as a means of achieving greater political power and influence, enabling them to advocate for policies that would improve the lives of themselves and their families.

The Women's Trade Union League (WTUL), founded in 1903, provided a platform for working-class women to organize and advocate for labor rights and suffrage. Led by figures like Mary Harris "Mother" Jones and Rose Schneiderman, the WTUL played a crucial role in mobilizing working-class women in support of suffrage and labor reform.

Challenges Faced by Marginalized Groups

Racism and Exclusion

Despite their contributions to the suffrage movement, women of color faced discrimination and exclusion from many mainstream suffrage organizations. Some white suffragists, particularly in the South, were reluctant to embrace interracial cooperation, fearing that it would undermine their efforts to secure suffrage for white women.

As a result, many African American suffragists were forced to organize separately from white suffrage organizations, forming their own clubs and associations to advance their goals. This division weakened the overall effectiveness of the suffrage movement and perpetuated racial divisions within the broader struggle for equality.

Class Bias and Elitism

Similarly, working-class women often found themselves marginalized within the suffrage movement, which was dominated by middle- and upper-class white women. Many suffrage organizations focused primarily on legislative advocacy and lobbying, neglecting the concerns and priorities of working-class women who were more focused on economic justice and labor rights.

This class bias and elitism within the suffrage movement created tensions and divisions that hindered efforts to build a more inclusive and diverse coalition. Working-class women were often excluded from leadership positions and decision-making processes, further marginalizing their voices and experiences within the movement.

Intersectional Activism and Solidarity

Despite these challenges, women of color and working-class women persisted in their activism, forging alliances and solidarity across lines of race, class, and gender. They organized their own suffrage clubs and associations, held mass meetings and rallies, and published newspapers and pamphlets to educate and mobilize their communities.

These intersectional efforts laid the groundwork for future social justice movements, demonstrating the power of solidarity and collective action in challenging systems of oppression and inequality. While the suffrage movement may have fallen short of its ideals of inclusivity and equality, the contributions of women of color and working-class women left an enduring legacy that continues to inspire and empower activists today.

Conclusion

The Women's Suffrage Movement was a diverse and multifaceted struggle, shaped by the intersecting identities and experiences of women from all walks of life. Women of color and working-class women played a vital role in the movement, contributing their voices, talents, and leadership to the fight for equality.

Despite facing racism, sexism, and class bias within the suffrage movement itself, these women persisted in their activism, forging alliances and solidarity across lines of race, class, and gender. Their efforts laid the groundwork for future social justice movements and helped to shape the broader struggle for equality in the United States.

As we reflect on the intersectionality within the suffrage movement, we are reminded of the importance of centering marginalized voices and experiences in our efforts to build a more just and equitable society. The legacy of women of color and working-class women in the suffrage movement serves as a powerful reminder of the ongoing work that remains to be done in the fight for justice and equality for all.

Chapter 6: State-by-State Campaigns

The struggle for women's suffrage in the United States was not a monolithic, nationwide movement but rather a series of state-by-state campaigns that unfolded over several decades. In this chapter, we will examine the state-by-state campaigns for suffrage and the varying degrees of success in different regions, as well as analyze the strategies used to secure suffrage at the state level.

The Patchwork of State Suffrage Laws

The journey towards women's suffrage in the United States was characterized by a patchwork of state suffrage laws, with each state adopting its own approach to extending voting rights to women. Some states embraced suffrage early on, while others resisted change until the very end. The process of securing suffrage at the state level was often arduous and contentious, requiring suffragists to navigate complex political landscapes and overcome entrenched opposition.

Early Successes: Wyoming and the West

The Western states emerged as early pioneers in the fight for women's suffrage, with Wyoming leading the way as the first state to grant women the right to vote in 1869. Inspired by the spirit of equality and democracy that characterized the frontier, Wyoming lawmakers passed a suffrage bill as part of a broader package of progressive reforms.

Following Wyoming's lead, other Western states, including Colorado, Utah, and Idaho, soon followed suit, enacting suffrage laws that extended voting rights to women. In these states, suffragists capitalized on the region's progressive ethos and the egalitarian values of frontier society to build support for suffrage and secure legislative victories.

Challenges in the East and South

In contrast to the Western states, suffrage campaigns in the Eastern and Southern regions of the United States faced greater resistance and opposition from entrenched interests and conservative forces. In the Eastern states, suffragists encountered skepticism and hostility from traditional power brokers, who viewed suffrage as a threat to the existing political order.

In the South, suffrage campaigns were further complicated by the legacy of slavery and racial segregation, which divided white and black women along racial lines and impeded efforts to build interracial coalitions. Suffragists in the South faced not only political opposition but also violence and intimidation from white supremacist groups who sought to maintain white supremacy and disenfranchise African Americans.

Strategies for Securing State Suffrage

Grassroots Organizing

One of the most effective strategies employed by suffragists in their state campaigns was grassroots organizing, mobilizing supporters at the local level to build momentum and pressure lawmakers to act. Suffragists established suffrage clubs and associations in communities across the country, holding meetings, organizing rallies, and engaging in door-to-door canvassing to recruit supporters and generate enthusiasm for the cause.

Lobbying and Legislative Advocacy

In addition to grassroots organizing, suffragists engaged in lobbying and legislative advocacy to advance their goals at the state level. They lobbied state legislatures and governors, urging lawmakers to pass suffrage bills and enact reforms that would extend voting rights to women. Suffragists also worked to elect sympathetic candidates to political office, believing that a friendly political climate was essential for achieving their objectives.

Public Education and Awareness

Suffragists recognized the importance of public opinion in shaping policy decisions, and they undertook extensive public education campaigns to raise awareness about the need for women's suffrage. They organized lectures, public meetings, and debates to educate the public about the benefits of extending suffrage to women and to counter opposition to suffrage.

Legal Challenges and Test Cases

In some states, suffragists pursued legal challenges and test cases to secure suffrage rights through the courts. They filed lawsuits challenging discriminatory voting laws and practices, arguing that such laws violated women's constitutional rights to equal protection and due process. While these legal challenges were often met with resistance from the judiciary, they helped to raise awareness about the injustices faced by women and contributed to the broader struggle for suffrage.

Conclusion

The state-by-state campaigns for suffrage in the United States were marked by a complex interplay of factors, including regional differences, political dynamics, and social attitudes. While some states embraced suffrage early on, others resisted change until the very end, requiring suffragists to employ a variety of strategies and tactics to secure legislative victories.

Despite the challenges and setbacks they faced, suffragists persisted in their efforts, building alliances, mobilizing supporters, and challenging the status quo in pursuit of equality and justice. Their grassroots organizing, lobbying efforts, and legal challenges laid the groundwork for the eventual passage of the 19th Amendment, which granted women the right to vote nationwide.

As we reflect on the state-by-state campaigns for suffrage, we are reminded of the importance of persistence, resilience, and collective action in advancing social change. The legacy of the suffrage movement serves as a testament to the power of ordinary individuals to effect meaningful change and to shape the course of history.

Chapter 7: Suffrage and the Progressive Era

The Women's Suffrage Movement was not an isolated phenomenon but rather a vital part of the broader progressive reform movement that swept across the United States during the late 19th and early 20th centuries. In this chapter, we will explore the connection between the suffrage movement and other progressive causes of the era, including labor rights and temperance, and examine how suffragists leveraged these connections to advance their cause.

The Progressive Movement and Social Reform

The Progressive Era, which roughly spanned from the 1890s to the 1920s, was characterized by a widespread belief in the need for social, political, and economic reform to address the challenges of industrialization, urbanization, and social inequality. Progressive reformers sought to tackle a wide range of issues, including labor rights, child labor, public health, education, and political corruption, in pursuit of a more just and equitable society.

Suffrage and Progressive Causes

Labor Rights

One of the key connections between the suffrage movement and other progressive causes of the era was the shared commitment to labor rights and workers' rights. Many suffragists recognized the importance of economic justice and empowerment for women, and they saw suffrage as a means of achieving greater political power and influence to advocate for labor reform.

Suffragists often collaborated with labor activists and unions to advance their shared goals, joining forces in campaigns for minimum wage laws, workplace safety regulations, and the eight-hour workday. They saw suffrage as a tool for amplifying the voices of working-class women and ensuring that their concerns were represented in the halls of power.

Temperance

Another area of overlap between the suffrage movement and other progressive causes was the temperance movement, which sought to reduce or eliminate alcohol consumption in society. Many suffragists were active supporters of temperance, viewing alcohol as a destructive force that undermined family stability and social order.

Suffragists saw suffrage as a means of advancing temperance goals, believing that women's votes could be used to promote laws and policies that would restrict or prohibit the sale and consumption of alcohol. They argued that women, as guardians of the home and family, had a vested interest in combating the social ills associated with alcohol abuse and addiction.

Leveraging Connections for Change

Coalition Building

Suffragists recognized the power of coalition building in advancing their cause and sought to forge alliances with other progressive groups and organizations. They worked closely with labor unions, temperance groups, and social reform organizations to build a broad-based coalition in support of suffrage and other progressive causes.

By aligning themselves with other reform movements, suffragists were able to amplify their message, pool their resources, and mobilize support from diverse constituencies. They saw suffrage as a common goal that transcended individual interests and ideologies, uniting progressives of all stripes in a shared quest for social justice and equality.

Using Suffrage as a Platform for Change

Suffragists also recognized the potential of suffrage as a platform for advancing broader social and political reforms. They argued that women's votes could be used to advocate for policies that would improve the lives of women and children, promote public health and education, and combat political corruption and injustice.

By framing suffrage as a means of achieving broader progressive goals, suffragists were able to garner support from a wider range of allies and constituencies. They positioned themselves as champions of social reform and used suffrage as a rallying cry to mobilize support for their cause.

Conclusion

The Women's Suffrage Movement was an integral part of the broader progressive reform movement that swept across the United States during the Progressive Era. Suffragists recognized the interconnectedness of social, political, and economic issues and sought to leverage their connections with other progressive causes to advance their own goals.

By collaborating with labor activists, temperance advocates, and social reformers, suffragists were able to build a broad-based coalition in support of suffrage and other progressive reforms. They saw suffrage as a means of achieving greater political power and influence to advocate for social justice, economic equality, and political reform.

As we reflect on the connection between suffrage and the progressive era, we are reminded of the power of collective action and coalition building in effecting meaningful change. The legacy of the suffrage movement serves as a testament to the enduring importance of solidarity, activism, and perseverance in the fight for a more just and equitable society.

Chapter 8: Suffrage and World War I

The outbreak of World War I in 1914 marked a watershed moment in the history of the Women's Suffrage Movement in the United States. As the nation mobilized for war, suffragists seized the opportunity to leverage the war effort to further their cause and gain public support for women's suffrage. In this chapter, we will explore the impact of World War I on the suffrage movement and analyze how suffragists utilized the war effort to advance their goals.

The Impact of World War I on the Suffrage Movement

Shift in Public Perception

World War I brought about a significant shift in public perception towards women's roles and capabilities, as women across the country stepped into traditionally male-dominated roles to support the war effort. With millions of men serving in the military, women took on jobs in factories, offices, and farms, filling essential roles previously held by men.

This unprecedented participation in the workforce challenged traditional gender norms and stereotypes, demonstrating women's ability to contribute meaningfully to the economy and society. Suffragists seized upon this shift in public perception to argue for women's suffrage, framing it as a matter of fairness and justice for women who were shouldering the burdens of war alongside men.

Political Opportunity

The war also created new political opportunities for suffragists as policymakers sought to mobilize all segments of society in support of the war effort. Suffragists capitalized on this opportunity to press their demands for suffrage, framing it as a patriotic duty and a means of strengthening the nation's democratic ideals.

Suffragists argued that women's contributions to the war effort, both on the home front and in volunteer organizations like the Red Cross and YMCA, demonstrated their fitness for citizenship and their willingness to serve their country. They called on policymakers to recognize women's sacrifices and contributions by granting them the right to vote.

Suffragists' Strategies during World War I

Patriotic Rhetoric

Suffragists employed patriotic rhetoric to frame their demands for suffrage in terms of national loyalty and duty. They portrayed suffrage as a way for women to contribute to the war effort and support the nation's democratic principles. Suffragists participated in patriotic rallies, parades, and fundraisers, waving flags and banners emblazoned with slogans like "The Woman's Hour Has Struck" and "For Democracy at Home as Well as Abroad."

Service and Sacrifice

Suffragists highlighted women's service and sacrifice during the war as evidence of their readiness for citizenship. They pointed to the thousands of women who volunteered as nurses, ambulance drivers, and relief workers on the front lines and in military hospitals, as well as those who worked in munitions factories and shipyards to support the war effort.

Suffragists argued that women's contributions to the war effort demonstrated their patriotism and commitment to their country, deserving of recognition and reward in the form of suffrage rights. They called on policymakers to honor women's sacrifices by granting them the right to vote.

Political Pressure

Suffragists also exerted political pressure on policymakers to support suffrage by mobilizing public opinion and leveraging their connections with influential allies. They organized letter-writing campaigns, petition drives, and lobbying efforts to pressure lawmakers to pass suffrage legislation at the state and federal levels.

Suffragists also forged alliances with labor unions, social reform organizations, and other progressive groups to build a broad-based coalition in support of suffrage. They staged rallies, protests, and marches to draw attention to their cause and demonstrate the strength of their movement.

Achievements and Legacy

State Suffrage Victories

The wartime efforts of suffragists bore fruit in several states, where lawmakers responded to public pressure by passing suffrage legislation. In 1917, New York became the first Eastern state to grant women the right to vote, followed by other states like Michigan, South Dakota, and Oklahoma.

These state suffrage victories were significant milestones in the fight for women's suffrage and demonstrated the growing momentum and public support for suffrage across the country. Suffragists capitalized on these victories to press for further reforms and to build momentum for a national suffrage amendment.

Federal Suffrage Amendment

The culmination of suffragists' efforts during World War I came with the passage of the 19th Amendment to the United States Constitution in 1920, which granted women the right to vote nationwide. The amendment was the result of decades of tireless activism and advocacy by suffragists, who had seized upon the wartime opportunity to push for suffrage rights.

The passage of the 19th Amendment was a historic victory for the Women's Suffrage Movement and marked a significant step forward in the quest for gender equality and political representation in the United States. Suffragists' efforts during World War I had helped to lay the groundwork for this achievement, demonstrating the power of collective action, political pressure, and strategic advocacy in effecting meaningful change.

Conclusion

World War I had a profound impact on the Women's Suffrage Movement in the United States, providing suffragists with a unique opportunity to leverage the war effort to advance their cause and gain public support for suffrage. Suffragists' patriotic rhetoric, service and sacrifice, and political pressure tactics helped to shift public opinion and mobilize policymakers in support of suffrage rights.

The wartime efforts of suffragists laid the groundwork for the eventual passage of the 19th Amendment, which granted women the right to vote nationwide. Suffragists' achievements during World War I demonstrated the power of activism, advocacy, and coalition building in effecting meaningful social and political change. Their legacy continues to inspire activists today in the ongoing fight for equality and justice for all.

Chapter 9: The Final Push: Tactics and Strategies

The final push for a federal amendment granting women the right to vote represents the culmination of decades of tireless activism and advocacy by suffragists in the United States. In this chapter, we will examine the strategies, tactics, and sacrifices made by suffragists during this critical period, as they worked tirelessly to secure passage of the 19th Amendment to the United States Constitution.

Context of the Final Push

By the early 20th century, the Women's Suffrage Movement had gained significant momentum, with suffragists making significant strides at the state level. However, suffrage remained elusive on the federal level, as efforts to pass a constitutional amendment granting women the right to vote had stalled in Congress.

Frustrated by the lack of progress and emboldened by the momentum of the Progressive Era, suffragists intensified their efforts to secure suffrage rights for women nationwide. They mobilized supporters, organized rallies and marches, and lobbied lawmakers with renewed vigor, determined to overcome the final obstacles standing in their way.

Tactics and Strategies

National Woman's Party (NWP) Tactics

The National Woman's Party (NWP), under the leadership of Alice Paul, adopted a more confrontational approach to suffrage activism during the final push for a federal amendment. Drawing inspiration from the tactics of the British suffragettes, NWP members engaged in acts of civil disobedience, picketing, and hunger strikes to draw attention to their cause and pressure lawmakers to act.

One of the NWP's most iconic actions was the picketing of the White House, which began in January 1917 and continued for over two years. Dressed in suffragist white and carrying banners with slogans like "Mr. President, How Long Must Women Wait for Liberty?" and "Kaiser Wilson," NWP members braved rain, snow, and public hostility to demand suffrage. Despite facing arrest, violence, and imprisonment, the picketers remained steadfast in their commitment to the cause, refusing to back down until their demands were met.

National American Woman Suffrage Association (NAWSA) Strategies

The National American Woman Suffrage Association (NAWSA), led by Carrie Chapman Catt, pursued a more conventional approach to suffrage activism during the final push for a federal amendment. Recognizing the need to work within the existing political system, NAWSA focused on lobbying Congress and building support for suffrage at the state level.

NAWSA employed a combination of legislative advocacy, public education, and grassroots organizing to advance the suffrage cause. They lobbied lawmakers, organized public meetings and rallies, and engaged in door-to-door canvassing to build support for suffrage among lawmakers and the public.

Grassroots Mobilization

Both the NWP and NAWSA relied heavily on grassroots mobilization to build support for suffrage during the final push for a federal amendment. Suffragists organized suffrage clubs and associations in communities across the country, holding meetings, distributing literature, and recruiting supporters to the cause.

Grassroots activists played a crucial role in generating public support for suffrage and pressuring lawmakers to act. They organized petition drives, letter-writing campaigns, and voter registration efforts to demonstrate the breadth and depth of support for suffrage among ordinary Americans.

Sacrifices and Challenges

Violence and Repression

Suffragists faced violence, harassment, and repression during the final push for a federal amendment, as opponents of suffrage sought to intimidate and silence them. NWP picketers were subjected to arrest, physical assault, and imprisonment, with some enduring hunger strikes and force-feeding in prison.

Even NAWSA activists faced threats and intimidation from anti-suffrage forces, particularly in states where suffrage campaigns were contentious. Suffragists risked their safety and well-being to fight for their rights, enduring hardship and sacrifice in pursuit of justice and equality.

Personal Sacrifice

Suffragists made personal sacrifices during the final push for a federal amendment, putting their careers, reputations, and even their lives on the line for the cause. Many suffragists faced social ostracism, professional setbacks, and personal hardship as a result of their activism, yet they remained steadfast in their commitment to the cause.

Suffragists like Alice Paul, Carrie Chapman Catt, and Lucy Burns dedicated their lives to the suffrage movement, sacrificing personal relationships, financial security, and personal comfort in pursuit of their goals. Their leadership, courage, and determination inspired generations of women to join the fight for equality and justice.

Legacy and Impact

The final push for a federal amendment granting women the right to vote culminated in the passage of the 19th Amendment to the United States Constitution in 1920, a historic victory for the Women's Suffrage Movement. The amendment enshrined women's right to vote in the Constitution, affirming their status as full and equal citizens under the law.

The tactics, strategies, and sacrifices made by suffragists during the final push for suffrage laid the groundwork for future social justice movements and helped to shape the course of American history. Their courage, resilience, and perseverance continue to inspire activists today in the ongoing fight for equality and justice for all.

Chapter 10: The 19th Amendment

The passage of the 19th Amendment to the United States Constitution in 1920 marked a historic milestone in the Women's Suffrage Movement, granting women the right to vote nationwide. In this chapter, we will delve into the ratification process, the final passage of the 19th Amendment, and examine the immediate aftermath and implications of women gaining the right to vote.

Overview of the Ratification Process

Congressional Approval

The journey towards the 19th Amendment began in Congress, where suffragists lobbied lawmakers and built support for suffrage legislation. After decades of advocacy and activism, Congress finally passed the 19th Amendment on June 4, 1919, following years of intense pressure and public debate.

The amendment, which stated that "the right of citizens of the United States to vote shall not be denied or abridged by the United States or by any State on account of sex," was hailed as a major victory for the Women's Suffrage Movement and a significant step forward in the quest for gender equality and political representation.

Ratification by the States

With congressional approval secured, the 19th Amendment was sent to the states for ratification, where it faced a final hurdle before becoming law. Ratification required approval by three-fourths of the states, or 36 out of 48 states at the time, a formidable challenge given the entrenched opposition to suffrage in some regions.

Suffragists launched a nationwide campaign to secure ratification, mobilizing supporters, organizing rallies and marches, and lobbying state lawmakers with renewed vigor. Their efforts paid off as state after state ratified the amendment, with Tennessee becoming the 36th and final state to do so on August 18, 1920.

Examination of the Immediate Aftermath

Celebration and Jubilation

The ratification of the 19th Amendment was met with widespread celebration and jubilation across the country, as suffragists and their supporters rejoiced in their hard-won victory. Women took to the streets in cities and towns across the nation, waving flags and banners, singing songs, and cheering for their newfound right to vote.

The passage of the 19th Amendment was hailed as a triumph of democracy and a testament to the power of grassroots activism and collective action in effecting meaningful social change. Suffragists, who had fought tirelessly for decades to secure suffrage rights for women, were finally able to see their efforts come to fruition.

Voter Registration Drives

In the immediate aftermath of the passage of the 19th Amendment, suffragists wasted no time in organizing voter registration drives and educational campaigns to encourage women to exercise their newly acquired right to vote. Suffragists set up tables outside polling places, distributed voter registration forms, and held informational meetings to teach women about their rights and responsibilities as voters.

These voter registration drives played a crucial role in empowering women to participate in the political process and ensuring that their voices were heard in elections. Women from all walks of life, including suffragists, activists, and ordinary citizens, eagerly registered to vote, eager to make their mark on history.

Implications of Women Gaining the Right to Vote

Political Empowerment

The passage of the 19th Amendment had profound implications for women's political empowerment, granting them a voice and a seat at the table in the democratic process. Women, who had long been excluded from political participation, were now able to vote for candidates who represented their interests and concerns, and to hold elected officials accountable for their actions.

Women's suffrage transformed the political landscape in the United States, ushering in a new era of female political engagement and activism. Women ran for office, served in government, and became leaders in their communities, making significant contributions to public policy and governance at all levels of government.

Social and Cultural Shifts

The passage of the 19th Amendment also brought about significant social and cultural shifts, challenging traditional gender roles and expectations and expanding the boundaries of women's rights and opportunities. Women's suffrage empowered women to assert themselves in new ways, challenging stereotypes and breaking down barriers to equality and opportunity.

Women's participation in the political process helped to shape public opinion and influence social change on a wide range of issues, from labor rights and civil rights to reproductive rights and environmental protection. Women's voices were increasingly heard and respected in the public sphere, paving the way for future generations of women to assert their rights and demand equality.

Conclusion

The passage of the 19th Amendment was a watershed moment in American history, marking the culmination of decades of struggle and sacrifice by suffragists in the Women's Suffrage Movement. The ratification of the amendment transformed the political landscape, granting women the right to vote and empowering them to participate fully in the democratic process.

The immediate aftermath of the passage of the 19th Amendment was marked by celebration and jubilation, as suffragists and their supporters rejoiced in their hard-won victory. Women wasted no time in exercising their newly acquired right to vote, participating in voter registration drives and educational campaigns to ensure that their voices were heard in elections.

The implications of women gaining the right to vote were far-reaching, shaping the course of American history and laying the groundwork for future social and political change. Women's suffrage empowered women to assert themselves in new ways, challenging stereotypes and breaking down barriers to equality and opportunity.

As we reflect on the legacy of the 19th Amendment, we are reminded of the power of grassroots activism, collective action, and perseverance in effecting meaningful social change. The passage of the 19th Amendment was a testament to the courage, resilience, and determination of suffragists who fought tirelessly for equality and justice for all.

Chapter 11: Challenges and Achievements After Suffrage

The passage of the 19th Amendment granting women the right to vote in 1920 marked a significant milestone in the Women's Suffrage Movement. However, the fight for gender equality did not end with suffrage. In this chapter, we will explore the challenges faced by women after gaining suffrage rights, including voter suppression and gender discrimination, as well as examine the achievements and advancements made by women in politics and society.

Challenges Faced by Women After Suffrage

Voter Suppression

Despite the passage of the 19th Amendment, women, especially women of color, continued to face barriers to voting in the form of voter suppression tactics. Poll taxes, literacy tests, and discriminatory voter registration practices were used to disenfranchise women, particularly women from marginalized communities.

African American women in the South, in particular, faced systematic voter suppression through tactics such as poll taxes, literacy tests, and intimidation by white supremacist groups. These barriers prevented many African American women from exercising their newly acquired right to vote, undermining the promise of suffrage for all women.

Gender Discrimination

Gender discrimination remained pervasive in American society, limiting women's opportunities and access to resources in various spheres of life. Women faced discrimination in employment, education, and political participation, as well as in access to healthcare and reproductive rights.

In the workplace, women were often paid less than their male counterparts for performing the same work and were excluded from many professions and leadership positions. In politics, women faced challenges in gaining equal representation and access to political power, with men dominating elected offices and policymaking roles.

Achievements and Advancements Made by Women

Political Representation

Despite the challenges they faced, women made significant strides in political representation and leadership in the years following suffrage. Women began to run for and win elected offices at all levels of government, from local school boards to the United States Congress.

In 1932, Hattie Wyatt Caraway of Arkansas became the first woman elected to the United States Senate, paving the way for future generations of women to serve in the Senate. In subsequent decades, women continued to break barriers in politics, with Shirley Chisholm becoming the first African American woman elected to Congress in 1968 and Nancy Pelosi becoming the first woman Speaker of the House in 2007.

Women's Rights Movements

The Women's Suffrage Movement laid the groundwork for future women's rights movements, inspiring activists to continue the fight for gender equality and social justice. In the decades following suffrage, women's rights movements emerged to address a wide range of issues, including reproductive rights, workplace equality, and violence against women.

The feminist movement of the 1960s and 1970s, often referred to as the Second Wave of feminism, brought renewed attention to women's rights and helped to catalyze significant advancements in gender equality. The movement pushed for legislative reforms, such as the passage of Title IX in 1972, which prohibited gender discrimination in education, and the passage of the Equal Rights Amendment (ERA), which sought to guarantee equal rights under the law regardless of sex.

Social and Cultural Change

Women's increased visibility and participation in public life helped to challenge traditional gender norms and stereotypes, reshaping social and cultural attitudes towards women and gender roles. Women's voices were increasingly heard and respected in the public sphere, as they advocated for their rights and fought for social change.

The women's movement of the 1960s and 1970s sparked a cultural revolution, challenging patriarchal institutions and promoting women's autonomy and self-determination. Women's increased presence in the workforce, politics, and media helped to challenge traditional notions of femininity and masculinity, paving the way for greater gender equality and diversity in society.

Conclusion

The passage of the 19th Amendment granted women the right to vote but did not eliminate the challenges and obstacles they faced in achieving full equality. Women continued to confront voter suppression, gender discrimination, and inequality in various spheres of life, even after gaining suffrage rights.

Despite these challenges, women made significant strides in political representation, leadership, and activism in the years following suffrage. They broke barriers, challenged stereotypes, and fought for their rights, laying the groundwork for future generations of women to achieve even greater advancements in gender equality and social justice.

As we reflect on the challenges and achievements after suffrage, we are reminded of the ongoing struggle for gender equality and the importance of collective action and advocacy in effecting meaningful social change. The legacy of the Women's Suffrage Movement continues to inspire women and men around the world to work towards a more just and equitable society for all.

Chapter 12: Legacy of the Suffrage Movement

The Women's Suffrage Movement in the United States was not just a moment in history but a transformative force that reshaped the fabric of American society and laid the groundwork for future social and political movements. In this chapter, we will explore the lasting impact of the suffrage movement on women's rights and American society, and analyze how it paved the way for future social and political movements.

Transforming Women's Rights

Political Empowerment

Perhaps the most significant legacy of the suffrage movement is the political empowerment of women. The passage of the 19th Amendment granted women the right to vote, giving them a voice and a seat at the table in the democratic process. Women began to exercise their newfound political power, participating in elections, running for office, and shaping public policy on issues that mattered to them.

The political empowerment of women has had far-reaching implications for American democracy, helping to diversify the political landscape and amplify the voices of women in government. Women's participation in politics has led to the enactment of laws and policies that promote gender equality, reproductive rights, and social justice, contributing to a more inclusive and representative democracy.

Legal and Social Rights

The suffrage movement also paved the way for advancements in women's legal and social rights. Inspired by the fight for suffrage, women's rights activists continued to push for reforms in areas such as reproductive rights, workplace equality, and access to education and healthcare.

The feminist movement of the 1960s and 1970s, often referred to as the Second Wave of feminism, built upon the achievements of the suffrage movement to advocate for greater gender equality and social justice. The movement helped to secure legislative victories, such as the passage of Title IX in 1972, which prohibited gender discrimination in education, and the passage of the Equal Rights Amendment (ERA), which sought to guarantee equal rights under the law regardless of sex.

Shaping American Society

Challenging Gender Norms

The suffrage movement challenged traditional gender norms and stereotypes, reshaping social and cultural attitudes towards women and gender roles. Suffragists asserted women's right to participate fully in public life and challenged the notion that women's place was solely in the home.

The movement sparked conversations about women's rights and autonomy, inspiring women to assert themselves in new ways and demand equal treatment and opportunities in all aspects of life. The increased visibility and participation of women in public life helped to challenge traditional notions of femininity and masculinity, paving the way for greater gender equality and diversity in American society.

Promoting Social Justice

The suffrage movement was not just a fight for women's rights but a broader struggle for social justice and equality. Suffragists recognized the interconnectedness of social, political, and economic issues and sought to address systemic injustices that affected women and marginalized communities.

Suffragists were often at the forefront of other progressive causes, such as labor rights, temperance, and civil rights, leveraging their connections with other social reform movements to advance their own goals. The suffrage movement served as a catalyst for broader social and political change, inspiring future generations of activists to fight for justice and equality for all.

Paving the Way for Future Movements

Intersectional Activism

The suffrage movement laid the groundwork for future social and political movements by demonstrating the power of intersectional activism and coalition building. Suffragists recognized the importance of solidarity and collaboration across different social movements and worked alongside other progressive groups to advance their shared goals.

The principles of intersectionality and inclusivity championed by suffragists continue to resonate in modern social justice movements, as activists advocate for the rights and dignity of all marginalized communities. The legacy of the suffrage movement serves as a reminder of the importance of building broad-based coalitions and working together to achieve meaningful social change.

Inspirational Leadership

The suffrage movement also provided a model of inspirational leadership and grassroots activism that continues to inspire activists today. Suffragists like Susan B. Anthony, Elizabeth Cady Stanton, and Sojourner Truth demonstrated the power of courage, resilience, and determination in the face of adversity, inspiring future generations of women and men to fight for justice and equality.

The legacy of the suffrage movement lives on in the ongoing struggle for gender equality, civil rights, and social justice around the world. Suffragists' achievements serve as a reminder of the power of collective action, advocacy, and perseverance in effecting meaningful social change, inspiring activists to continue the fight for a more just and equitable society for all.

Conclusion

The legacy of the suffrage movement is profound and far-reaching, shaping the course of American history and inspiring social and political movements around the world. The movement transformed women's rights, empowered women to participate fully in public life, and challenged traditional gender norms and stereotypes.

The suffrage movement paved the way for future social and political movements by demonstrating the power of intersectional activism, coalition building, and inspirational leadership. Suffragists' achievements continue to inspire activists today in the ongoing fight for justice and equality for all, reminding us of the enduring importance of courage, resilience, and determination in the quest for a more just and equitable world.

Chapter 13: Global Perspectives on Women's Suffrage

The fight for women's suffrage was not confined to the borders of the United States but was part of a broader global movement for gender equality and political rights. In this chapter, we will compare the suffrage movement in the United States to similar movements around the world, examining how the American suffrage movement influenced global efforts for women's rights.

The Suffrage Movement in the United States

Historical Context

The Women's Suffrage Movement in the United States emerged in the 19th century as women began to agitate for greater political rights and representation. Influenced by the principles of democracy and equality, suffragists fought tirelessly for the right to vote, organizing rallies, marches, and protests to demand suffrage rights.

Key figures in the American suffrage movement included Susan B. Anthony, Elizabeth Cady Stanton, and Sojourner Truth, who played instrumental roles in advancing the cause of women's rights and mobilizing support for suffrage.

Strategies and Tactics

American suffragists employed a variety of strategies and tactics to advance their cause, including lobbying lawmakers, organizing public demonstrations, and engaging in civil disobedience. Suffragists used petitions, lectures, and publications to raise awareness about the importance of women's suffrage and to build support for their demands.

The suffrage movement in the United States was characterized by both radical and moderate factions, with organizations like the National Woman's Party (NWP) adopting more confrontational tactics, such as picketing the White House, while organizations like the National American Woman Suffrage Association (NAWSA) focused on legislative advocacy and grassroots organizing.

Global Suffrage Movements

United Kingdom

The suffrage movement in the United Kingdom, often referred to as the suffragette movement, emerged in the late 19th century and was led by figures like Emmeline Pankhurst and her daughters, Sylvia and Christabel Pankhurst. Suffragettes in the UK employed militant tactics, including hunger strikes, arson, and vandalism, to draw attention to their cause and pressure lawmakers to act.

The suffragette movement culminated in the passage of the Representation of the People Act in 1918, which granted voting rights to women over the age of 30 who met certain property qualifications. Full suffrage rights were granted to women over the age of 21 in 1928.

New Zealand

New Zealand became the first self-governing country in the world to grant women the right to vote in 1893, following a sustained campaign led by suffragists like Kate Sheppard. The suffrage movement in New Zealand was characterized by non-violent protest and political organizing, culminating in the passage of the Electoral Act in 1893, which granted women the right to vote in parliamentary elections.

New Zealand's suffrage victory served as a model for other countries around the world and inspired suffragists in other nations to continue their fight for women's rights.

Australia

The suffrage movement in Australia was closely linked to the broader struggle for democratic reforms and social justice. Suffragists like Vida Goldstein and Louisa Lawson played key roles in advocating for women's suffrage, organizing rallies, petition drives, and public meetings to build support for their cause.

Women in South Australia gained the right to vote in 1894, followed by women in Western Australia in 1899. By 1908, women in all Australian states had won the right to vote in federal elections, making Australia one of the earliest countries to grant women full suffrage rights.

Influence of the American Suffrage Movement

Inspiration and Collaboration

The American suffrage movement served as a source of inspiration and collaboration for suffragists around the world. Suffragists in other countries looked to the United States for inspiration and guidance, studying American suffrage tactics and strategies and drawing on the experiences of American suffragists to inform their own activism.

American suffragists also collaborated with their counterparts in other countries, exchanging ideas, resources, and support to advance the cause of women's rights on a global scale. Suffragists like Alice Paul and Carrie Chapman Catt were instrumental in promoting international solidarity and cooperation among women's rights activists.

Global Impact

The American suffrage movement had a profound impact on global efforts for women's rights, helping to catalyze broader social and political changes around the world. The passage of the 19th Amendment in the United States inspired suffragists in other countries to redouble their efforts and intensified pressure on governments to grant women the right to vote.

The success of the suffrage movement in the United States helped to legitimize the demand for women's suffrage on the international stage, paving the way for future advancements in women's rights and gender equality. American suffragists' achievements served as a beacon of hope and inspiration for women's rights activists around the world, fueling their determination to continue the fight for justice and equality.

Conclusion

The suffrage movement in the United States was part of a broader global struggle for gender equality and political rights. American suffragists inspired and collaborated with their counterparts in other countries, helping to advance the cause of women's rights on a global scale.

The legacy of the suffrage movement continues to resonate in the ongoing fight for gender equality and social justice around the world. The achievements of American suffragists served as a catalyst for broader social and political changes, inspiring future generations of activists to continue the fight for a more just and equitable world for all.

Chapter 14: Unfinished Business: Continuing Struggles for Equality

While significant progress has been made in the fight for gender equality in the United States, there remains unfinished business as we continue to grapple with persistent challenges and barriers to full equality for women. In this chapter, we will explore the ongoing struggles for equality faced by women in the United States, as well as examine contemporary movements and initiatives aimed at addressing these challenges.

Persistent Challenges to Gender Equality

Gender Pay Gap

One of the most pressing challenges facing women in the United States is the gender pay gap, which continues to persist despite decades of activism and legislative efforts. Women, on average, earn less than men for performing the same work, with women of color experiencing even greater disparities in pay compared to white men.

The gender pay gap not only perpetuates economic inequality but also undermines women's financial security and contributes to broader social and economic disparities. Closing the gender pay gap requires addressing systemic factors such as occupational segregation, discrimination, and lack of access to family-friendly workplace policies.

Representation in Leadership

Women remain underrepresented in leadership positions across various sectors, including politics, business, and academia. Despite making up half of the population, women hold fewer than 30% of seats in Congress, account for only a small percentage of Fortune 500 CEOs, and are significantly underrepresented in positions of leadership in academia and other fields.

The lack of representation in leadership perpetuates gender inequality by limiting women's influence and decision-making power in shaping policies and practices that affect their lives. Increasing women's representation in leadership requires addressing barriers such as gender bias, systemic discrimination, and lack of support for women's advancement.

Gender-Based Violence

Gender-based violence, including domestic violence, sexual assault, and harassment, remains a pervasive problem in the United States, affecting women of all ages, races, and socioeconomic backgrounds. Despite increased awareness and efforts to address gender-based violence, many survivors continue to face barriers to accessing support and justice.

Gender-based violence not only inflicts physical and psychological harm on survivors but also perpetuates cycles of trauma and perpetuates gender inequality. Addressing gender-based violence requires comprehensive strategies that prioritize prevention, survivor support, and accountability for perpetrators.

Contemporary Movements and Initiatives

MeToo Movement

The #MeToo movement, which emerged in 2017 as a grassroots social media campaign, has sparked a national reckoning with sexual harassment and assault in the United States. The movement has empowered survivors to speak out about their experiences, hold perpetrators accountable, and demand systemic change to end gender-based violence.

The #MeToo movement has led to increased awareness and scrutiny of sexual harassment and assault in various sectors, including politics, entertainment, and the workplace. It has also prompted organizations and policymakers to implement reforms aimed at preventing and addressing sexual misconduct and creating safer environments for all.

Equal Pay Advocacy

Advocates and organizations continue to push for policies and initiatives aimed at closing the gender pay gap and promoting pay equity in the United States. Efforts to address the gender pay gap include advocating for legislation such as the Paycheck Fairness Act, which aims to strengthen protections against pay discrimination and promote greater transparency in pay practices.

Employers and businesses are also taking steps to address pay equity within their organizations, including conducting pay audits, implementing salary transparency policies, and offering salary negotiation training for employees. These efforts are aimed at promoting greater accountability and fairness in compensation practices and ensuring that women are paid equitably for their work.

Women's Political Leadership

There is a growing movement to increase women's representation in political leadership roles in the United States, with organizations like Emily's List, She Should Run, and VoteRunLead working to recruit, train, and support women candidates for elected office. Efforts to elect more women to political office are aimed at diversifying political leadership, amplifying women's voices in policymaking, and advancing women's rights and priorities.

In addition to electoral activism, there is also a push for structural reforms, such as campaign finance reform and electoral system reforms, to address barriers to women's political participation and create a more inclusive and equitable political landscape.

Conclusion

The fight for gender equality in the United States is far from over, as we continue to grapple with persistent challenges and barriers to full equality for women. The gender pay gap, lack of representation in leadership, and gender-based violence are just a few of the issues that require urgent attention and action.

Contemporary movements and initiatives, such as the #MeToo movement, equal pay advocacy, and efforts to increase women's political leadership, are helping to advance the cause of gender equality and drive meaningful change. By amplifying women's voices, challenging systemic barriers, and advocating for policy reforms, we can work towards a more just and equitable society where all women can thrive and fulfill their potential.

Chapter 15: Conclusion: Looking Forward

As we reflect on the legacy of the suffrage movement and the journey towards gender equality in the United States, it is clear that progress has been made, but there is still much work to be done. In this concluding chapter, we will reflect on the progress made since the suffrage movement and the work that still needs to be done, and issue a call to action for continued advocacy and activism in the fight for gender equality.

Reflection on Progress

Advancements in Women's Rights

Since the passage of the 19th Amendment in 1920, women in the United States have made significant strides in the fight for gender equality. Women have gained access to education, entered the workforce in greater numbers, and broken barriers in fields traditionally dominated by men.

Women's political representation has also increased, with more women serving in elected office at all levels of government. Women have been elected to positions of leadership in Congress, state legislatures, and local governments, shaping policies and advocating for issues that affect women and marginalized communities.

Cultural Shifts and Awareness

The suffrage movement and subsequent women's rights movements have brought about significant cultural shifts and increased awareness of gender inequality and discrimination. Issues such as the gender pay gap, gender-based violence, and workplace harassment have gained greater attention and scrutiny, sparking public discourse and prompting action to address these issues.

The #MeToo movement, in particular, has empowered survivors to speak out about their experiences and demand accountability for perpetrators of sexual harassment and assault. It has also led to increased awareness and understanding of the pervasiveness of gender-based violence and the need for systemic change to end it.

Challenges and Unfinished Business

Gender Pay Gap

Despite advancements in women's rights, significant challenges remain, including the gender pay gap. Women continue to earn less than men for performing the same work, with women of color experiencing even greater disparities in pay compared to white men.

Closing the gender pay gap requires addressing systemic factors such as occupational segregation, discrimination, and lack of access to family-friendly workplace policies. Efforts to promote pay equity must include measures to ensure transparency in pay practices, strengthen protections against pay discrimination, and address barriers to women's advancement in the workforce.

Representation in Leadership

Women remain underrepresented in leadership positions across various sectors, including politics, business, and academia. Despite making up half of the population, women hold fewer than 30% of seats in Congress, account for only a small percentage of Fortune 500 CEOs, and are significantly underrepresented in positions of leadership in academia and other fields.

Increasing women's representation in leadership requires addressing barriers such as gender bias, systemic discrimination, and lack of support for women's advancement. Efforts to promote diversity and inclusion in leadership must be accompanied by structural reforms to address systemic inequities and create pathways for women's leadership and advancement.

Gender-Based Violence

Gender-based violence, including domestic violence, sexual assault, and harassment, remains a pervasive problem in the United States. Despite increased awareness and efforts to address gender-based violence, many survivors continue to face barriers to accessing support and justice.

Addressing gender-based violence requires comprehensive strategies that prioritize prevention, survivor support, and accountability for perpetrators. Efforts to end gender-based violence must include investments in prevention programs, support services for survivors, and legal reforms to strengthen protections and improve access to justice.

Call to Action

Continued Advocacy and Activism

As we look forward, it is clear that the fight for gender equality is far from over. We must continue to advocate for policies and initiatives that promote gender equity, challenge systemic barriers, and create opportunities for women and girls to thrive.

We must support efforts to close the gender pay gap, increase women's representation in leadership, and end gender-based violence. We must also work to address intersectional inequalities and prioritize the needs and experiences of women of color, LGBTQ+ individuals, and other marginalized communities.

Engage in Collective Action

Achieving gender equality requires collective action and collaboration across sectors and communities. We must come together to amplify women's voices, advocate for policy reforms, and hold institutions and decision-makers accountable for advancing gender equity.

We must support grassroots organizations, community-based initiatives, and advocacy campaigns that are working to address gender inequality and create a more just and equitable society for all.

Educate and Empower

Education and awareness are key to driving meaningful change and challenging societal norms and attitudes that perpetuate gender inequality. We must educate ourselves and others about the root causes of gender inequality and the ways in which it manifests in our lives and communities.

We must empower women and girls to assert their rights, pursue their aspirations, and advocate for change. We must also engage men and boys as allies in the fight for gender equality, challenging harmful stereotypes and promoting healthy and respectful relationships.

Conclusion

As we look forward, let us recommit ourselves to the unfinished work of the suffrage movement and the ongoing fight for gender equality. Let us build on the progress made, confront the challenges that remain, and work together to create a future where all individuals, regardless of gender, can live with dignity, respect, and equality.

By continuing to advocate, educate, and empower, we can create a more just and equitable world for future generations. Let us seize this moment to reaffirm our commitment to gender equality and work towards a future where every person has the opportunity to thrive and fulfill their potential, regardless of gender.

Don't miss out!

Visit the website below and you can sign up to receive emails whenever Michael Johnson publishes a new book. There's no charge and no obligation.

https://books2read.com/r/B-A-OREFB-QHYAD

BOOKS 2 READ

Connecting independent readers to independent writers.

Did you love *The Women's Suffrage Movement:*? Then you should read *The Industrial Revolution*[1] by Michael Johnson!

"Explore the seismic shift that reshaped America's economy in 'The Industrial Revolution: Transforming America's Economy.' From the birth of industry to the rise of modern capitalism, this book traces the evolution of American society through technological innovation, urbanization, and economic expansion. Discover the social, environmental, and cultural impacts of industrialization, and reflect on its enduring legacy in shaping the world we live in today. A riveting narrative of progress, upheaval, and the enduring quest for innovation, 'The Industrial Revolution' illuminates the roots of America's economic power."

1. https://books2read.com/u/31JPyW

2. https://books2read.com/u/31JPyW

About the Author

Michael Johnson is a distinguished historian specializing in American history. With a degree in History from Harvard University, Johnson's work delves into pivotal moments, figures, and themes shaping the United States. He has authored numerous acclaimed books, offering insightful perspectives and engaging narratives. Johnson's commitment to meticulous scholarship and compelling storytelling has earned him widespread acclaim in the field. Passionate about sharing his expertise, he frequently engages in lectures and public events to foster a deeper appreciation for America's past.